BRITAIN IN OLD P

RAF CHIVENOR

D A V I D   W A T K I N S

ALAN SUTTON PUBLISHING LIMITED

Alan Sutton Publishing Limited
Phoenix Mill · Far Thrupp · Stroud
Gloucestershire · GL5 2BU

First published 1995

*Cover photographs: (front) Hunter F.6s of the
'Black Dragons' aerobatic team make a
formation turn, 1963; (back) the technical and
domestic site, 1953.*
*Title-page photograph: formatting over Lundy
Island in 1982, the Hawks of No. 151(R)
Squadron celebrate the victory in the Falkland
Islands by spelling out the station name with
their tail codes. (BAe)*

British Library Cataloguing in Publication Data.
A catalogue record for this book is available from
the British Library.

ISBN 0–7509–1034–8

Typeset in 9/10 Sabon.
Typesetting and origination by
Alan Sutton Publishing Limited.
Printed in Great Britain by
Ebenezer Baylis, Worcester.

No. 547 Squadron flew from Chivenor from December 1942 to May 1943 with
Wellington VIIIs. A detachment to Tain to carry out torpedo training was made during
the spring of 1943, before converting to Wellington XIs. The aircraft depicted is one of
the squadron's Wellington XIIIs in early 1943. (J. Bryant)

Introduction

Situated on the North Devon coast between Exmoor and the River Taw, Royal Air Force station Chivenor can arguably claim to be the most ideally sited of all the UK's airfields. The station also enjoys a good weather record and an excellent relationship with the local community – a relationship which was suitably demonstrated on 17 April 1963 when it was granted the Honorary Freedom of the Borough of Barnstaple. The name of the airfield is derived from the original site of a 13th-century Saxon settlement, Chyvenor(e) – Ciffa's bank or shore.

The importance of the location of an airfield at Chivenor was first recognized within an ambitious scheme to make Barnstaple an important aviation centre, presented to the Chamber of Commerce in May 1938. Together with plans to build a barrage across the River Taw to retain enough water to accommodate flying boats, consideration was given to the likely importance of the area in the event of war. The arguments for an airfield included its central position for the 'Empire' (sic), good land communications, good meteorological record, immunity from air attack, distance from any industrial centre, and low cost. Many of these factors were taken into account two years later when the site was chosen as a Coastal Command base and, although only built for 'the duration of the present emergency', Chivenor subsequently played an important role in the wartime battle against the U-Boats in the Atlantic and the training of generations of pilots for both Coastal and Fighter Command.

Having survived post-war uncertainty and the reduction of RAF strength, the station's infra-structure changed very little until the late 1970s owing to the Air Ministry's reluctance to accept its permanence. Nonetheless, with the coming of jet aircraft, concrete hardstandings were constructed in 1952, together with a new control tower the following year. In August 1966, work started on the building of 208 airmen's married quarters on a 19 acre site adjoining the existing twenty houses which had been built after the war.

One unit to have recorded uninterrupted service at Chivenor since 1958 is the search and rescue unit, 'A' Flight, No. 22 Squadron. The work of the helicopter unit is a story in its own right. Many of its daring rescues, sometimes in the most appalling conditions, have gone largely unnoticed by the public; since 1958 some thirty-seven awards for bravery have been presented to members of the helicopter crews, including three of the Air Force Cross, four of the Air Force Medal, a George Medal, and thirteen Queen's Commendations.

The indecent haste with which the station was closed in 1995 was occasioned by the end of the Cold War and the anticipated reduction of the

RAF's training requirements. By transferring all Hawk training to RAF Valley, the Ministry of Defence and the Treasury preferred, yet again, to place its trust in an isolated Welsh base.

Chivenor had previously survived many threats of closure since the mid-1950s, including its proposed use as a guided missile base in 1957. Its period of inactivity between 1974 and 1980 meant a loss of important revenue for the local economy which, estimated at £2 million in 1974, had risen to £22 million by 1995. The worst to suffer were the local charities who had benefited from some of the proceeds of the annual air days, which had raised £102 5s 8d from the first in September 1945 to over £10,000 from the last in July 1993.

Despite the uproar and protests when the closure was first announced in January 1993, only the briefest mention was deemed necessary when the final flying course graduated in September 1994 and the last two Hawks were flown away in the following March. The transfer of the base to the Royal Marines on 1 October 1995 not only closed a chapter on the RAF's history, but also marked the end of its close and happy association with the people of North Devon.

So how did it all begin? The use of a small grass field near Heanton Court, $4^{1}/_{2}$ miles west of Barnstaple, was first discussed by the Barnstaple Chamber of Commerce in May 1932, and the successful visit of Sir Alan Cobham's Flying Circus the following year prompted its use as a permanent aerodrome. A licence for the Barnstaple & North Devon Flying Club, equipped with two de Havilland Gypsy Moths, was granted in November 1933 and Heanton was officially opened as the Barnstaple & North Devon Airport on 13 June 1934. A daily service to Lundy Island was inaugurated by the Atlantic Coast Air Services in April 1935, with aircraft including a de Havilland Dragon, a General Aircraft Monospar, and Short Scion passenger aircraft.

It was at this time that the first RAF aircraft landed at the airfield: a Hawker Audax (K2003) of the School of Photography at Heanton for ten days during August 1934, tasked with a photographic survey of Exmoor.

On 26 April 1937, the company's name was changed to that of the Lundy & Atlantic Coast Airlines. The following year, the flying club was selected as a centre for subsidized, basic flying instruction within the Civil Air Guard scheme, with the first member qualifying for his 'A' licence that September. In May 1939, Western Airways began to use Barnstaple Airport as a link in its service between Swansea and Penzance.

At the outbreak of war all civilian flying ceased and the airfield was requisitioned under Emergency Regulations. Over 2,200 return flights to Lundy had been made during the six years of accident-free civilian flying at Heanton. The ground side of Lundy & Atlantic Coast Airlines was embodied within the Ministry of Aircraft Production as a Civilian Repair Unit: between June 1940 and May 1944 the unit was contracted to repair RAF and RN Tiger Moths, at its peak averaging an output of thirty aircraft per month.

In February 1940, plans by the Air Ministry to construct an aerodrome on the site led to the purchase of land adjoining the original grass airfield. Owned by Sir William Williams, this land included Marsh Farm and the whole of Chivenor Farm, which was farmed by the Reed brothers. Two months later, the contract for £172,000 was awarded to the firm of George Wimpey. Building work started in May with the first of the officers' lines, followed on 21 June by the construction of the first of the three 3,000 ft runways and associated taxiways, together with four Bellman and four Hinaidi type hangars.

RAF Chivenor opened on 25 October 1940 as a training base within No. 17 Group, Coastal Command, becoming operational the following month with the formation of No. 3 (Coastal) Operational Training Unit, flying Beauforts and Ansons. On 1 December the unit was joined by No. 252 Squadron from Bircham Newton to convert from Blenheims to Beaufighters. The conversion was slow, hampered by both poor aircraft serviceability and the heavy snowfall of February 1941.

By the end of 1940, the domestic arrangements were complicated by the fact that neither the officers' nor sergeants' messes had been completed, which meant that they had to be billeted out. However, with the eventual opening of messes in early January 1941, the station building programme was virtually completed.

During December 1940, KLM/BOAC began to use Chivenor as a staging post for their Bristol–Lisbon run, operating DC.2s, and DC.3s. A representative from BOAC had arrived at Chivenor on 13 December to organize the necessary ground support and Customs officials to enable their aircraft to use the airfield as a refuelling point, as the aircraft were unable to take off from Whitchurch with full fuel loads. The first aircraft, a DC.3 G-AGBE piloted by Mr Parmentier and carrying seven passengers, landed at Chivenor on Christmas Eve 1940. Distinguished passengers who used the facilities at Chivenor during 1941 included cabinet minister Clement Attlee, the US Republican party leader, Wendell Wilkie, and the Japanese ambassador, Mr Shingenitsn. One notable flight involved KLM DC.3 G-AGBB which was shot down by Ju 88s over the Bay of Biscay on 1 June 1943 with the loss of seventeen passengers, including actor Leslie Howard. The service was continued until February 1944, when BOAC's main wartime base was moved from Bristol to Hurn and the flights through Chivenor were terminated.

By December the station was now considered fully operational, and on the 31st twenty pilots from No. 42 Squadron arrived for an operational conversion course, which was followed by the start of No. 1 (Beaufort) Course on 13 January 1941. In early 1941 the main runway was extended at both ends, and the construction of this, together with associated taxiways and hard standings, was well under way when the two flying units were moved away and replaced by detachments of various Coastal Command units and No. 5 (C) OTU, which formed on 1 August 1941 to train Beaufort and Anson crews in the anti-shipping role. Casualties on the unit were high because of the Beaufort's troublesome Bristol Centaurus VI engines, which compelled the diversion of all available improved Taurus XII engines to the unit. Some fifteen courses were held at Chivenor before No. 5 (C) OTU was transferred to Turnberry in early 1942.

The airfield was attacked by the Luftwaffe four times during early 1941. During March, a low-level attack by two Heinkel He IIIs injured three airmen, but fortunately most of the bombs failed to explode. The most serious raid was at 0300 hrs on 16 April when four He IIIs damaged seventeen aircraft, the control tower and the runways during a 30 minute raid and rendered the airfield out of action for several days. Houses in nearby Braunton were also damaged. Two more raids during May were a nuisance only and caused no damage. Because of the vulnerability to air attack, some 150 airmen and soldiers from the 70th Battalion, Queen's Regiment (Young Soldiers Battalion), which had been attached for aerodrome defence duties, were provided with sleeping accommodation off the station by requisitioning Wrafton Rectory, Chivenor Cottage, St Brannock's Hall and the Masonic Hall, Braunton.

A 'War Weapons week' was held in Barnstaple during late April 1941, which included a march-past of fifty airmen from Chivenor, followed by a special church parade. The event coincided with the first operational flight from the airfield when five Blenheims from No. 21 Squadron arrived on 4 April for a shipping sweep off the French coast. Two 500 ton trawlers were successfully attacked, despite one of the Blenheims being damaged by return fire.

A surprise visitor arrived on the airfield on 20 November 1941 in the shape of Ju 88A–5 M2+MK c/n 6073 of 1/*Kustenfliegergruppe* 106, normally based at Morlaix in France. Because of the effects of the British 'Meacon' radio counter-measures, the young and inexperienced crew, which included *Uffz* Herms, *Obergefrs* Krautter and Kurz, and *Gefr* Klein, became lost during a sortie over the Irish Sea and mistook the North Devon coast for France. Sighting Chivenor's flarepath, the enemy bomber landed at 2130 hrs and was captured by a party of quick-thinking RAF airmen under the command of Sqn Ldr 'Len' Harvey, with the crew taken prisoner. The slightly damaged aircraft was put on show to the general public at North Walk, Barnstaple, before being fitted with the tailplane from an Anson and flown to Farnborough on 12 December, as HM509. It was eventually operated by No. 1426 (Enemy Aircraft) Flight at Duxford and returned to Chivenor in October 1942 as part of a 'circus' of captured enemy aircraft, which gave flying and ground demonstrations. It returned to Chivenor again the following month to provide fighter affiliation training for the Beaufighters of No. 235 Squadron. It was during one of these exercises that it was responsible for the loss of one of the 'attacking' aircraft, when a Beaufighter stalled and crashed on the shore of the River Taw at nearby Instow. The Ju 88 was eventually struck off charge in June 1944.

During the first two years of the war, German and Italian submarines had been able to sink over 3,000,000 tons of Allied shipping in the Atlantic while operating from French ports in the Bay of Biscay. Whereas daylight attacks by Coastal Command aircraft against the U-Boats had limited success, attacks at night were virtually impossible – which was used to advantage by the submarines, at their most vulnerable as they surfaced to recharge their batteries. Therefore an idea by Sqn Ldr H. de V. Leigh, a 90 cm search light to illuminate the target – the 'Leigh Light' – was developed at the Coastal

Command Development Unit. Used in conjunction with improved ASV radar, the Leigh Light showed promise. As a result, on 8 January 1942 No. 1417 Flight was formed at Chivenor to train crews in the use of Leigh Light-equipped Wellington GR.VIII bombers under the command of Sqn Ldr J.H. Greswell. The unit was renumbered No. 172 Squadron during April and became operational on 3 June. On the same night a squadron Wellington attacked and badly damaged the Italian submarine *Luigi Torrelli* near Santander. Success eventually came to the squadron on 5 July when American Pt Off W.B. Howell straddled *U–502* with depth charges as it was crash-diving. The submarine sank with all hands and Howell was subsequently awarded the DFC for his actions.

Between November 1941 and October 1942 the Wellingtons were augmented by detachments of Whitley bombers of Nos 51, 77 and 502 Squadrons, the latter making Coastal Command's first ASV 'kill' on 30 November 1941 when Fg Off Holdsworth (in Whitley Z9190 YG–T) attacked *U–206* in the Bay of Biscay.

During the 197 operational patrols flown by the three resident squadrons in the first month (June 1942) as an operational Coastal Command station, Chivenor's aircraft made nine attacks against U-boats, resulting in only one damaged submarine but with the loss of five Whitleys and one Wellington. These aircraft had been shot down by patrolling Luftwaffe fighters, so the Beaufighters of Nos 235, 236 and 248 Squadrons and No. 404 RCAF Squadron were based at Chivenor between July 1942 and April 1943 to offer essential long-range protection.

From March 1943, further Wellington squadrons were posted to Chivenor to counter the anticipated increase of U-boat attacks in the Bay of Biscay. These included Nos 14, 36, 179, 304 (Polish), 407 RCAF, 547 and 612 Squadrons. Seven U-boats were sunk during 1943, with another three in the lead-up to the D-Day invasion in June 1944.

Another unit to operate from the station during this period was No. 748 (Naval OTU) Squadron, RNAS, from St Merryn. Equipped with nine Seafires, the unit provided fighter affiliation training for the Wellingtons from September 1943 to February 1944.

Following disastrous flooding of the aerodrome during September 1943, it was decided to carry out essential drainage work near the hangars, while at the same time constructing a perimeter track to the south of the airfield and re-surfacing the main runway. This major work necessitated the temporary transfer of the major part of No. 172 Squadron to Gibraltar and Nos 407 and 612 Squadrons to St Eval, leaving only a maintenance echelon at Chivenor.

With the return of the Wellington squadrons by January 1944, a definite build-up and preparation for the forthcoming invasion of France was noticeable. Although operational flying was not stepped up, an increase in the number of enemy fighters operating over the Bay of Biscay led to the loss of several Wellingtons. The station sick quarters was also extended to accommodate the expected heavy casualties during the initial stages of the fighting; plans were made to fly some of the wounded soldiers direct to Chivenor from the battlefield, but fortunately never needed to be put into operation.

Although the English Channel had been effectively sealed against U-boats for the Allied invasion, *U–441* was sighted by a Wellington of No. 304 Squadron on 18 June, some 50 miles from Brest. Piloted by Flt Lt Antoniewicz, the Wellington (HF338/A) straddled the submarine with six depth charges, sinking it with all hands. A second U-boat was noted at the scene, but managed to crash-dive before an attack could be made. The total time of the operation from sighting to the explosions had been a mere three minutes!

During June 1944, Chivenor's Wellingtons had flown some 359 operational sorties, with seven attacks on U-boats resulting in one sinking and four confirmed as damaged. On the debit side, five aircraft were reported as missing.

Chivenor's U-boat successes began to decline after the invasion of France, with the final 'kill' by a Wellington of No. 407 Squadron, RCAF occurring in the Bay of Biscay on 30 December 1944. The station's contribution to the U-boat war should not be underestimated: between November 1941 and December 1944, Chivenor's Whitleys and Wellingtons were responsible for sinking fifteen U-boats and damaging a further fourteen. Bad weather, engine failures, attacks by enemy fighters and return fire from the U-boats all contributed to the risks undertaken by the crews during their regular and generally monotonous eight-hour ASW patrols, and consequently twenty-one Whitleys and eighty-eight Wellingtons were lost while operating from the station. During the period September 1941 to June 1945, some three DSOs, twenty-five DFCs, five DFMs and one AFC were awarded to Chivenor aircrew, with a further seventy-four personnel receiving a Mention in Despatches.

An example of the price paid by the crews occurred on 27 August 1944, when a No. 172 Squadron Wellington flown by Flt Lt George Whitley was hit by the return fire from a U-boat it had attacked near the mouth of the Gironde, which damaged the port engine. Crashing into the sea, the four survivors, including the Canadian navigator, Fg Off Roderick Grey, scrambled for a solitary, one-man dinghy. Despite losing part of his own leg, Grey helped two of his injured friends into the dinghy and spent the rest of the night clinging to its side; at dawn his friends found him dead. The three survivors were eventually rescued by a Sunderland some fifteen hours later. For his courage and selfless sacrifice, Fg Off R.B. Grey was posthumously awarded the George Cross.

With the decrease of U-boat activity during the spring of 1945, the last operational sortie was flown from Chivenor by a Wellington of No. 407 Squadron, RCAF on 2 June 1945. The remaining Wellington squadrons were either disbanded or transferred to other stations.

Post-war uncertainty over the future of Chivenor saw a miscellany of meteorological and anti-aircraft units in residence. These included the Halifaxes and Fortresses of Nos 517 and 521 Squadrons, which flew regular ten-hour, 600 mile sorties over the Atlantic and Bay of Biscay gathering important weather information; the Mosquitos of No. 248 Squadron and the Beaufighters of No. 254 Squadron (which constituted the remnants of the

RAF's anti-shipping strike wings); and the Spitfires and Martinets of No. 691 (AAC) Squadron.

In October 1946, the station was transferred to No. 11 Group, Fighter Command, and, a year later, No. 203 Advanced Flying School arrived from Keevil with Spitfires, Harvards and Martinets. The unit was responsible for providing pilots destined for operational squadrons with three months of tactical training in the day fighter role or with fighter/reconnaissance training. Course training began on 15 October 1947.

With the transfer of the AFS to Stradishall in July 1949, the station was occupied by Nos 5 and 7 (AAC) Squadrons, and No. 1 Overseas Ferry Unit, which moved in from Manston in July 1950. The ferry unit's duties included not only the delivery of Mosquitos and Meteor and Vampire jets to the Middle East, but also the ferrying of the first Vampires to the Far East when, between November 1950 and January 1951, forty-four aircraft were flown from Chivenor to Singapore.

A station flight was formed for the first time at Chivenor in February 1950, equipped with a handful of Tiger Moths and Buckmasters. The flight was short-lived, however, disbanding during the August following the crash of a Buckmaster in a field adjoining the airfield the previous month.

Post-war civilian flying was resumed at Chivenor during June 1950 after the RAF's decision to allow the newly formed Wrafton Flying Club to lease a corner of the airfield, close to Wrafton railway station. The club erected some buildings on the site and became known as the Puffin Aero Club, and in August the pre-war airmail service to Lundy Island was revived using a de Havilland Rapide. The venture unfortunately failed and the aircraft was repossessed, but in December 1952 the air service was recommenced by Devonair Ltd, with two Austers. Although civil flying effectively ceased at Chivenor in August 1955 with the loss of Devonair's Autocrat in the Bristol Channel, the air service was never considered fully economic and, despite being renamed the North Devon Flying Club in 1959, was sold the following year.

The necessity for an increased supply of fighter pilots to serve in the Korean War saw No. 229 Operational Conversion Unit transferring from Leuchars in March 1951. Equipped with de Havilland Vampire FB.5s and Meteor T.7s, the OCU had formed some three months earlier and provided sixty hours of tactical training for pilots in the day fighter role. Air-to-air firing at targets towed by Beaufighters, Tempests and, later, Mosquitos and Meteors was carried out on ranges off the North Devon coast and the Gower Peninsula. A firing range off Hartland Point was later used.

With the completion of No. 41 Course in April 1954, the Vampires were briefly replaced by Canadair Sabres, which brought a taste of supersonic flying to Chivenor until May 1955, when deliveries of Hunter fighters had been established and the first training course could begin. For the next three years, until Hunter trainers became available, the Vampires found a new role in grading the student pilots before they progressed to Hunters. In June 1955 the work of the OCU was augmented by the formation of the Fighter/Recce Flight, issued with a handful of Meteor F.8s.

The first mention of 'shadow squadron' status being allocated to the Chivenor Hunters was during Exercise 'Vigilant' in May 1957, when six aircraft of No. 127 (Reserve) Squadron were detached to Valley. Although ostensibly a 'paper' unit, No. 127 Squadron came into existence again during Exercise 'Iron Bar' the following November, being joined by the newly formed No. 131 (Reserve) Squadron in October 1958; the following month they were renumbered as No. 234 (Reserve) and No. 145 (Reserve) Squadrons respectively. During further identity changes, 145 Squadron was transferred to the Lightning OCU at Middleton St George in June 1963 and replaced by No. 63 (Reserve) Squadron, while No. 79 (Reserve) Squadron was formed in January 1967 for the training of fighter/recce pilots, pilot attack instructors, and instrument rating examiners.

The most notable event of Chivenor's post-war era occurred in March 1967, when the tanker *Torrey Canyon* went aground on the Seven Stones Reef, 16 miles off Lands End, spilling its cargo of crude oil. For three days Chivenor's Hunters dropped napalm to try to burn off the oil during a joint RAF/RN operation. Also in 1967, the OCU achieved a unique peacetime record when it completed the training of the 2,000th pilot for Fighter Command.

In August 1969, a permanent detachment of four Hunters and pilots was constituted at Gibraltar for 'Defence of the Rock' duties, the role being passed to Chivenor following the disbandment of the West Raynham Hunter squadrons.

The final Hunter unit to be based at Chivenor was the Singapore Operational Training Flight, which was formed in November 1972 and attached to the station for weaponry training. With an establishment of three Hunter F.74Bs and two Hunter T.75As, the flight was a component of the Singapore Air Defence Command and moved to Brawdy in August 1974.

On 30 August 1974, No. 229 OCU was transferred to Brawdy in South Wales, where it was immediately renamed No. 2 Tactical Weapons Unit. The station was left on a 'Care and Maintenance' basis, and a holding party was retained to look after the service families from Cyprus who were temporarily housed in the married quarters.

Three years later, in October 1977, it was revealed that the Ministry of Defence was actively considering a future use for the base, which was supported the following spring by a further MoD announcement that a second TWU would be needed because of the increased requirement for pilots' weapons training.

In May 1979 it was officially announced that, following an extensive rebuilding programme, the station was to be re-activated on 1 August 1980 with the return of No. 2 TWU, flying BAe Hawk T.1s. Comprising Nos 63 and 151 (Reserve) Squadrons, the unit commenced operation on 7 August with the training of fast-jet pilots in the art of air-to-air combat, weaponry and tactical low flying, as well as providing pre-OCU courses for navigators.

Under the government's 1992 'Options For Change' policy, both resident training squadrons were renumbered as Nos 19 and 92 (Reserve) Squadrons, and on 1 April the station was transferred from RAF Strike Command to Support Command; consequently, No. 2 TWU became No. 7 Flying Training School. In conjunction with RAF Valley, the old TWU course was also replaced by the new Mirror Image Training Course, with courses separated into two phases totalling some 100 hours of advanced and tactical training. The first true 'mirror image' course (CV01) was able to commence, with four students, during September 1992.

Helicopter search and rescue operations at Chivenor go back to June 1957 with the arrival of the Sycamore HR.14s of 'E' Flight, No. 275 Squadron. On 8 November 1958, the Sycamores were replaced by the Whirlwind HAR.4s of 'A' Flight, No. 22 Squadron, which was transferred from St Mawgan. From that date, and flying a succession of Whirlwind HAR.10s, Wessex HC.2s and Sea King HAR.3 helicopters, the flight has carried out many rescue operations in an area covering the south-west of England, South Wales and Somerset. With the advent of the more sophisticated Sea Kings in late 1994, the area of operations was increased to include mid-Wales and beyond Ireland. On 12 September 1988, 'A' Flight achieved its 4,000th rescue when two holidaymakers were airlifted from cliffs at Ilfracombe Bay.

Despite a £12 million rebuilding programme and a survey which confirmed the importance of the base, the government's 1993 Defence Estimate White Paper called for a decrease in the RAF's training requirements and further speculated that the future of Chivenor was under review. On 7 December 1993 it was announced officially that No. 7 FTS was to cease as a flying unit with the graduation of the final flying course on 30 September 1994, following which the numberplate of No. 19 (Reserve) Squadron would transfer to Valley and No. 92 (Reserve) Squadron would disband.

The last Hawk unit to operate from Chivenor was the weapons detachment from RAF Valley which, from October 1992, used the station as a forward operating base for its aircraft deploying to the Pembrey ranges, being administered by the Hawk Support Flight. Following completion of the building work at RAF St Athan, the No. 4 FTS Hawk detachment was transferred from Chivenor to the South Wales base in March 1995.

On Friday 17 March 1995, fifteen years of Hawk operations at Chivenor were ended with the low-key but emotional departure of the two remaining aircraft to Valley, flown by Sqn Ldrs Stu Robinson and Paul Adams. The station was closed for further flying on 24 March 1995, following the withdrawal of air traffic control. The Hawks' departure left only the Sea Kings of 'A' Flight, No. 22 Squadron in residence, together with No. 624 Volunteer Gliding School, which had moved from Exeter in June 1966 and successively operated Sedburgh, Cadet, Prefect, Venture and Vigilant gliders, providing basic flying training and passenger flying for air cadets.

The station was temporarily re-activated during May and September 1995 when BAe Harrier GR.7s from Wittering and Laarbruch, Germany, operated under canvas for exercises 'Hill Foil' and 'Hazel Flute', respectively. The intensive two-week exercises were part of the continuing Harrier force's work-up for service with the NATO Allied Rapid Reaction Force.

Following its final closure as an RAF base on 1 October 1995, the station was transferred to the Royal Marines for use by 3 Commando Logistics Regiment and 59 Independent Commando Squadron, RE from RM Coypool and Seaton Barracks, Plymouth.

A sight familiar to many who have passed through the gates of RAF Chivenor. This sign was erected in the 1980s to replace an original which featured the badges of the station's flying units. (Author)

The site of Heanton aerodrome on the estuary of the River Taw, late 1930s. The flying club's original buildings are visible, as is Chivenor Farm to the left of the photograph. In 1966 the land was developed, with the construction of the station's married quarters. (R.L. Knight Collection)

Looking east towards Barnstaple. The 500 acres of farmland to the left of the river were purchased by the Air Ministry in 1940 to build the airfield. (R.L. Knight Collection)

Short Scion 1 G-ACUW of Lundy & Atlantic Coast Air Services Ltd. Capable of carrying five passengers, the aircraft was purchased in April 1935 and made up to ten flights to Lundy every day. Impressed into RAF service as AV981 in May 1940, it was written off in a flying accident at Ringway the following November. (R.L. Knight Collection)

The opening ceremony of the Barnstaple & North Devon Airport, 13 June 1934. The mayor, Alderman Charles Dart, can be seen on a ladder in front of an Avro 504, G-ACCX. (R.L. Knight Collection)

The aerodrome's hangars and flying club in 1939, with Scion G-ACUW and DH.60 Gypsy Moth G-AAIM. The club's two flying instructors, Bob Boyd and Tommy Nash, provided members with training to qualify for their 'A' licence for £35. One of the flying club's early members was the author, Henry Williamson. (R.L. Knight Collection)

General Monospar ST.4 G-ACCP, which was purchased in 1938 and used for business charter flights, can be seen in front of the aerodrome's buildings. Some of these buildings are still in existence. (R.L. Knight Collection)

As part of his National Aviation Day Display tour, Sir Alan Cobham's Flying Circus visited Heanton in September 1933. Flown by Flt Lt Johnson, Handley Page Clive I G-ABYX provided passenger joyride flights for 7s 6d. (Anon)

An excellent photograph of Beaufort I X8931 of No. 2 Flight, No. 3 (C) OTU off the North Devon coast, 1941. (IWM)

No. 3 (Coastal) Operational Training Unit was formed in November 1940 for general reconnaissance crew training, equipped with Ansons, Beaufighters and Blenheims. This Beaufort I, N1113 of No. 1 Flight, was written off in June 1941. (Anon)

With the temporary disbandment of No. 3 (C) OTU in July 1941, its task was taken over by No. 5 (C) OTU. Two of the unit's Beaufort Is, L9812 and N1020, are seen at dispersal at Chivenor during 1941 or 1942. (Anon)

The station commander, Gp Capt J.H. Sadler, with the US Republican envoy, Mr Wendell Wilkie, during his stop-over visit at Chivenor, 5 February 1941. (RAF Chivenor)

Beaufighter Ic R2198 of No. 252 Squadron, early 1941. Although the squadron transferred to Chivenor in December 1940 to convert from Blenheims, problems prevented it from becoming operational until the following March. (MoD)

During the spring of 1941, No. 252 Squadron operated a mixture of Blenheim IFs and IVFs and Beaufighter Ics. The Beaufighter depicted (R2153) served with the squadron from January to March 1941, when it was transferred to No. 272 Squadron, also at Chivenor. (IWM)

Captured at Chivenor on 20 November 1941 after mistaking the North Devon coast for France, Ju 88A-5 M2+MK of *Ku. Fl. Gr.* 106 is seen with hastily applied RAF markings. The aircraft had earlier taken off from Morlaix in France with two other aircraft to attack shipping in the Irish Sea. (Anon)

Before being flown to Farnborough to join No. 1426 (Enemy Aircraft) Flight in December 1941, the captured Ju 88 was displayed to the general public at North Walk, Barnstaple, and later evaluated by Chivenor's pilots. (RAF Chivenor)

No. 612 (County of Aberdeen) Squadron, AAF flew Whitleys at Chivenor on anti-submarine patrols from May to June 1943, before converting to Wellingtons. (RAFM)

Typical of the Whitley crews of No. 612 Squadron at Chivenor during 1943 was (left to right) Billy Vennall, Bill Parsons, Johnny Ralph (later killed on the Berlin Airlift), Arthur Clutterbuck, Arthur Wood and Len McConnell. (Bill Parsons)

WAAF fabric workers and workshop hands clean and respray Whitley V Z9217 of No. 51 Squadron at Chivenor, 1942. (IWM)

A U-boat attack by a Whitley V, Z9228 of No. 51 Squadron, 1 August 1942. The aircraft arrived over the target after it had submerged and dropped six depth charges ahead of the swirl. Nothing further was seen, apart from some air bubbles, and the aircraft returned to base. (RAF Chivenor)

An aerial view of Chivenor, 6 January 1942. The villages of Wrafton and Braunton can be seen in the top left of the photograph. Some attempt to camouflage the airfield and runways with painted hedges is apparent. (MoD)

Chivenor, looking to the west, with at least thirty Wellingtons and Whitleys dispersed around the airfield, July 1942. In the foreground is Chivenor Farm, with the Barnstaple to Ilfracombe railway line skirting the northern edge. (RAFM)

Wellington VIII HX379 of No. 172 Squadron flying low over the sea, 28 October 1942. The 'stickleback' ASV aerials along the top of the fuselage and the retracted Leigh Light on the underside can clearly be seen. (RAFM)

Seen off the estuary of the Rivers Taw and Torridge, west of Chivenor, is Wellington GR.XIV HF113 of No. 172 Squadron, 1943. The aircraft served with the squadron

from May to October 1943, when it was transferred to No. 3 OTU at Haverfordwest. (Jeff Rounce)

Aircrew of No. 172 Squadron, autumn 1942. The CO, Wg Cdr Brolly, is seated with his pet dog and flanked by OC 'A' Flight, Sqn Ldr Thompson

Personnel of the Radar Training Flight, in front of a Wellington bomber. The flight was known to have been renamed as the

and OC 'B' Flight, Sqn Ldr Henderson. The aircraft is a dual-control Wellington Ic. (Jeff Rounce)

ASV Training Flight and was disbanded in June 1945. (RAF Chivenor)

In September 1943 a combination of high tides and poor airfield drainage caused extensive flooding, which severely hampered working conditions. The Wellington GR.XIV stranded in the hangar is MF134/G, probably from No. 1 Overseas Aircraft Preparation Unit. (RAF Chivenor)

More stranded Wellingtons in No. 7 Hangar, which is awash with water. Despite a considerable amount of drainage work, the airfield was flooded again in October 1945 when the sea wall was breached following exceptionally high tides. (RAF Chivenor)

Even the airman on the bicycle finds it difficult to negotiate the flooded roads. Some 8 acres of land were under water and it was several days before life on the station returned to normal and operations could resume. (RAF Chivenor)

Very little is known of this wartime photograph apart from its inscription: 'Fg Off Wadley and crew'. (RAF Chivenor)

B-26C Marauder 41-34715 of the 454th Bomb Squadron, 9th AF, was being ferried from Port Lyautey, Morocco, to St Eval on 4 June 1943 by 1st Lt Joe Patton. Crossing the English coast, the aircraft encountered bad weather and overshot an emergency landing at Chivenor, slewed off the runway and came to rest in a hedge. (USAF)

A Polish crew prepares a Wellington of No. 304 (Slaski) Squadron for an anti-submarine patrol. The squadron was based at Chivenor between February and September 1944, sinking two U-boats and damaging two more. (IWM)

The ASV radar scanner 'chin' housing, single Browning 0.303 in machine gun, and Polish insignia are evident on this Wellington of No. 304 Squadron. (IWM)

Sqn Ldr D.M. Brass and crew of No. 612 (County of Aberdeen) Squadron, AAF, Chivenor. Brass was later promoted to wing commander, leading the squadron from January 1944 to February 1945. (RAF Chivenor)

No. 304 Squadron's radio and radar section at Chivenor, 1944. (Sikorski Institute)

The original caption for this photograph of a Canadian crew walking away from Wellington XIV NB858 of No. 407 Squadron on 12 September 1944 states: 'This Demon crew is happy because they have completed their 13th mission without due mishap.' The actual sortie had flown a few days earlier in NB828! (RCAF)

The commanding officer of No. 172 Squadron, Wg Cdr S.R. Ramsey-Smith, and crew pose for the camera, 1944. Back row, left to right: Fg Off Colin Patterson (RAAF), CO, Flt Sgt 'Jacko' Jackson. Front row: Flt Sgts Ken Hogbin, Roberts, and Gavin Smith. (Ken Hogbin)

Wellington XIV NB908 of No. 36 Squadron, flown by WO Selwyn, suffered a port engine failure during a single-engined landing and collided with a stationary Hudson of No. 209 Squadron, 19 December 1944. (Andy Anderson)

A Wellington GR.XIV and aircrew of No. 36 Squadron with its commanding officer Wg Cdr G. Williams, early 1945. The parish church of Heanton Punchardon is on the hill in the background. (G.E. Jones)

(Left) RAF Chivenor, looking north across the River Taw, 7 August 1944. Forty-three Wellingtons of the three resident Coastal Command squadrons can be seen, together with two Martinets and a Halifax by the ATC tower. Work on the runway extensions is also visible. (Jeff Rounce)

During January 1945, North Devon experienced the worst snow since 1881, with drifts of 12 ft in places and even the River Taw being partially frozen over. Airmen worked hard to clear the airfield; here, snow is being brushed off a Wellington of No. 14 Squadron. (Anon)

Within a few days of the heavy snowfall which hit Chivenor in January 1945, the main runway was cleared to enable Wellington NB770 of No. 36 Squadron, flown by Flt Lt Look, to get airborne for a Channel search. (G.E. Jones)

Halifax III LV839 of No. 517 Squadron climbs out for a ten-hour 'Epicure' sortie over the Bay of Biscay to gather important weather data. (RAFM)

No. 517 Squadron flew its last 'weather flight' on 20 June 1946. The following day the crews posed for this disbandment photograph. (J. Rounce)

A Martinet (JN680) from No. 4 APC, Talbebby flown by Jeff Rounce on fighter affiliation training, October 1944. (J. Rounce)

With Lundy Island as a backdrop, Beaufighter TF.X RD438 of No. 254 Squadron carries a torpedo during a training flight from Chivenor, autumn 1945. (Wg Cdr D.T.M. Lumsden)

Between July 1945 and May 1946, No. 248 Squadron flew many exercises with the Home Fleet and also carried out rocket attacks on captured U-boats. Mosquito FB.VI RF610 was eventually sold to Yugoslavia in 1952. (RAFM)

Twelve Mosquito FB.VIs of No. 248 Squadron were detached to North Weald for the Battle of Britain Flypast over London, September 1945. (RAF Chivenor)

The Fortress IIIs of No. 521 Squadron were eventually grounded following the end of 'Lend Lease', which meant spares were difficult to obtain. The Fortresses were replaced by Halifax VIs in February 1946. (J. Rounce)

Crowds gather to watch the contingent from RAF Chivenor march through the Square in Barnstaple for the Victory Parade, 8 June 1946. Similar parades were held at Braunton, Bideford and Ilfracombe. (RAF Chivenor)

The Coastal Command Fighter Affiliation Training Unit, or 'Fitchew's FATU'. The unit operated Spitfires and Martinets in early 1946, and was commanded by Sqn Ldr E. Fitchew, DFC. (Sqn Ldr J.A. Forrest)

A Martinet of the CCFATU gets airborne for an air-to-air firing sortie with one of the resident fighter squadrons, early 1946. (Sqn Ldr J.A. Forrest)

Engine fitters service a Spitfire LF.XVIe, TB630, of No. 691 (AAC) Squadron, 1948. The unit was renumbered No. 17 Squadron the following year. (G.P. Young)

Seen visiting Chivenor during the summer of 1948 is Lancaster B.VII NX687 of the Empire Flying School, Hullavington. (Sqn Ldr Maurice Biggs)

One of the duties of the Spitfires of 'A' Flight, No. 5 Squadron, was to fly simulated low-level attacks for the Army. TE452 crashed during such a tactical exercise at Welcombe, Devon, in August 1950. (RAF Chivenor)

Martinet TT.1 JN647 was one of six aircraft used for target-towing duties by No. 203 AFS at Chivenor between October 1947 and July 1949. (Len Lineker)

No. 691 (AAC) Squadron moved to Chivenor in October 1946, equipped with Spitfires, Martinets and Harvards. The unit provided 'targets' for the Army gunners at Cleave, Watchet and Penhale. (RAF Chivenor)

Engine fitters at work again, with a Martinet (NR637) being prepared for another sortie; the target-towing winch is of note. The aircraft behind is Oxford T.2 NJ296. (G.P. Young)

A pleasing study of Spitfire LF.16e TE244 of the Gunnery Squadron, No. 203 AFS, flown by its OC and ex-Battle of Britain 'Ace', Sqn Ldr 'Mac' Mackenzie, 1947. (Wg Cdr K.W. Mackenzie)

No. 203 AFS ran nineteen courses for day fighter pilots at Chivenor before transferring to Stradishall in July 1949. The various canopies fitted to these Spitfire LF.16es are of interest. (J.D. Gibson via C.H. Thomas)

Resting between sorties is Spitfire LF.16e RW390, summer 1948. The aircraft was written off in a taxying accident later that year. (Sqn Ldr Maurice Biggs)

Six Spitfire PR.XIXs were used by No. 3 Squadron, No. 203 AFS for fighter/recce training. Seven of these courses were held at Chivenor for pilots destined for front-line squadrons. (J.D. Gibson via C.H. Thomas)

High over the North Devon countryside is Harvard T.2B FX443 of No. 203 AFS, 1948. (Gp Capt Norman Curtis)

The plaque says it all: 'Fighter Command Cup Winners; RAF Chivenor; 1947/8'. The captain of the rugby team was Sqn Ldr 'Mac' Mackenzie. (Wg Cdr K.W. Mackenzie)

Returning from another sortie, Spitfire LF.16e TD280 of No. 17 Squadron is marshalled between the hangars, 1948. (G.P. Young)

In July 1950, eight Spitfires of No. 17 Squadron masqueraded as Bf 109s for the RAF display at Farnborough, when they 'harassed' Mosquitos re-creating the wartime attack on Amiens prison. (Anon)

Beaufighter TT.10s of No. 17 Squadron, April 1949. Although the airframes were in good condition, the Beaufighters' Bristol Hercules engines caused great problems for the groundcrews. (G.P. Young)

Parked on the grass dispersal in front of the ATC tower is a Beaufighter TT.10 of 'B' Flight, No. 5 Squadron, summer 1950. Concrete aircraft-servicing platforms were laid down in 1952. (G. Coombes)

Beaufighter TT.10s of No. 5 Squadron at Chivenor, 1950. (J. Coombes)

During its stay at Chivenor, the Overseas Ferry Unit (OFU) was responsible for the ferrying of 147 aircraft. Its greatest task, however, was the ferrying of the first forty-four Vampire jets to the Far East, one of which is seen *en route* to Singapore in December 1950. (Bob Hillard)

The OFU transferred from Manston to Chivenor at short notice in July 1950 with a miscellany of aircraft, including Buckmaster I RP232. (RAF Chivenor)

Until the arrival of Vampire T.11s in January 1953, the OCU's students were provided with dual training in Meteor T.7s, such as VW473 pictured here. (Anon)

The arrival of the Vampires of No. 229 OCU from Leuchars in March 1951 necessitated the runway being lengthened to its present 2,000 yds. A Vampire FB.5 of the Tactical Flight is seen on the new ASP in 1953. (RAFM)

Between January 1951 and April 1954, No. 229 OCU was responsible for some forty-one Vampire courses. The instructors of 'A' Flight are seen here in September 1953 with their OC, Flt Lt Colin Sloan (fifth from left). (Colin Sloan)

The technical and domestic site, September 1953. The infamous black-painted wooden airmen's billets (or 'Lines') can be seen. Most were sold in the early 1970s. (RAF Chivenor)

On 4 September 1953, Pt Off Brian Cleathero was forced to bale out over farm land on Codden Hill, Bishops Tawton, when his Vampire suffered an engine failure. He is seen here inspecting the wreckage with officials at Cobbaton. (N.D. Museum)

Tempest TT.5 EJ660 of No. 229 OCU is shown here being flown by Fg Off B.N. Smith, 1953. (RAF Chivenor)

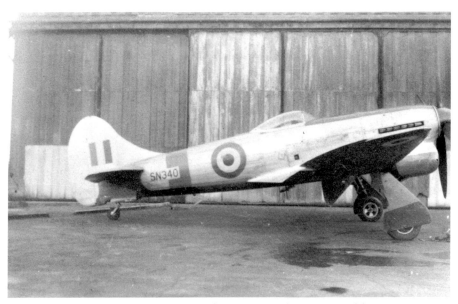

The Vampires carried out live air-to-air firing against drogues towed by Tempests over the Bristol Channel. This particular Tempest served with the OCU from October 1952 until November 1954. (Anon)

Seen landing on Runway 28/10 is Vampire FB.5, WA254, July 1956. The Vampires were retained until 1957 to provide students with twenty-six hours of tactical flying before they progressed to Hunters. (J.D. Rawlings)

Between April and November 1956 the OCU operated an additional nine Vampire courses. This Vampire was damaged beyond repair during an air firing exercise in April 1957. (J.D. Rawlings)

An idyllic setting for an airfield: Chivenor, looking to the west, taken from a Sycamore helicopter of No. 275 Squadron, 1958. The additional married quarters have yet to be built, while the prewar flying club buildings can be seen to the right. (George Francis)

The domestic site, 1950s. The officers' mess is in the foreground. Also visible are officers' quarters ('E' Lines), the airmen's quarters ('C' and 'D' Lines), the airmen's mess and club to the north of the sports field, and station HQ to the left of the field. (RAF Chivenor)

Vampire T.11 XD383, July 1956. The Vampire trainers were replaced by Hunter T.7s in October 1958. (J.D. Rawlings)

Vampire T.11 XE923 formed part of the static display at Chivenor's 'At Home' Day, September 1956. It was still wearing the codes of its previous owner, No. 226 OCU (Frank Davis)

Canadian-built Sabre F.4 XB741, soon after delivery, 1954. For twelve months this state-of-the-art day fighter formed the establishment of No. 229 OCU, which was the RAF's first swept-wing jet OCU. (AVM A.A. Case)

Three Sabre F.4s, September 1954. The nearest is from 'B' Flight, while the other two are from 'C' Flight. Six Sabre courses were held at Chivenor between August 1954 and March 1955. (Anon)

Three of the pilots to break the 'sound barrier' during the 1954 Open Day. Flt Lt Les Thorogood (centre), Fg Off Brian Smith (left) and Flt Lt Ian Gordon-Johnson both received the DFC and Air Medal and Oak Leaf Cluster respectively, for their services in Korea. (N.D. Museum)

Armourers service the 0.50 in calibre machine guns of a Sabre F.4 at Chivenor, 1954. (N.D. Museum)

Hunters were delivered to Chivenor in February 1955, with course training beginning the following May. Four Hunter F.1s are seen above Exmoor the same year. (AVM A.A. Case)

Hunter F.1 WT696 served with No. 229 OCU from November 1955 to July 1957. The advent of the bigger jets brought noise problems and the inevitable protests from local residents. (J.D. Rawlings)

Awaiting clearance for take-off is Hunter F.1 WW606. Pilots had to be conscious of the type's high fuel consumption and limited reserves, which restricted the sorties to thirty minutes. (J.D. Rawlings)

Seconds before touch-down is Hunter F.1 WW644. During almost three years of operations, the OCU lost only ten Hunter F.1s in flying accidents. (J.D. Rawlings)

The formation of the Fighter/Recce Flight in June 1955 saw three Meteors transferred from Stradishall and the start of the first course the following month. WH360 was one of the flight's Meteor F.8s (J.D. Rawlings)

Gp Capt H.P. Pleasance OBE, DFC, was the station commander from January 1956 to January 1958. One of his initiatives was the Planned Flying Programme to maximize aircraft utilization. (Gp Capt H.P. Pleasance)

No. 229 OCU's aircraft form an impressive display during the AOC's Parade, May 1956. They include Hunter F.4s, Vampire FB.5s, Meteor T.7s and F.8s, and Mosquito TT.35s. (Gp Capt H.P. Pleasance)

During the summer of 1956, No. 17 Course was responsible for the training of the first Luftwaffe officers, including Lt Col Wehnelt and Majs Barkhorn and Krupinski. (RAF Chivenor)

Air Cdre P.C. Mead, CBE, DFC, AFC, inspects the unit's Vampires during the AOC's inspection, May 1956. (RAF Chivenor)

No. 229 OCU was the first unit to receive the Hunter T.7. This beautiful shot of XL592 was taken in 1959, a year after it had been delivered to Chivenor. (MoD)

Passing over Lundy Island, Hunter T.7 XL579 wears the colours of No. 145 (Reserve) Squadron on its nose. It served at Chivenor from October 1958 to December 1965. (Sqn Ldr John Harvey)

A mixed formation of Hunter F.4s and T.7s, 1960. The lead Hunter wears the markings of No. 234 (Reserve) Squadron, while the others are from No. 145 (Reserve) Squadron. (RAF Chivenor)

The station sports day, 10 August 1960. Testing for anabolic steroids should prove unnecessary for this event! (RAF Chivenor)

Members of the 'Black Dragons' aerobatic team at the Battle of Britain Air Day, including Sqn Ldr E.C. Chandler, Flt Lts B.M. Burley and G.W. Timms, and Fg Off D.E. Dodd, September 1960. The solo aerobatic pilot was Flt Lt I.F. Weston. (RAF Chivenor)

Led by Sqn Ldr R.C. Wood, Hunter F.6s of the aerobatic team make a formation turn, 1963. (MoD)

A line-up of Hunter F.4s of No. 234 (Reserve) Squadron, 1960. The type was in use from May 1957 to June 1961. (RAF Chivenor)

Another mixed formation, comprising a Hunter F.4 and T.7 and a Meteor T.7. By this time the latter type had been relegated to target-towing duties for the Hunters. (RAF Chivenor)

Instructors and students examine the target banner for hits following an air-to-air firing exercise. (Sqn Ldr John Harvey)

'The bitterest snow-up in memory' was how the winter of 1963 was described, as blizzards and snow drifts of up to 20ft throughout January and February cut off many villages. With no flying possible, airmen make a giant snowball as part of their clearance operations. (RAF Chivenor)

During an impressive ceremony on Castle Green, the Mayor of Barnstaple, Stanley Woolaway, presents the Freedom Scroll to Chivenor's CO, Gp Capt D.W.B. Farrar, 15 April 1963. (RAF Chivenor)

The red Templar's crosses flanking the fuselage roundel denote that these Hunter F.4s are from No. 145 (R) Squadron. The three Meteor TT.(8)s belong to the Towed Target Flight. (RAF Chivenor)

Seen at the ROC Open Day in October 1962 is Hunter F.6 XG159 in the striking Royal Blue colour scheme of its former owner, No. 92 Squadron 'Blue Diamonds' aerobatic team. The No. 92 Squadron badge has been overpainted with that of No. 145 (R) Squadron. (Anon)

Five years later, and another Hunter wears the colours of No. 92 Squadron from its previous service in Germany. This T.7, XL571 'Queenie', eventually crashed in Wales during 1977. (Author)

Parked on No. 1 Squadron's ASP alongside the Type 'B' ATC tower are Hunter T.7s of No. 234 (R) Squadron. (George Raby)

On 28 March 1967, the tanker *Torrey Canyon* took a 'short cut' to catch the tide and hit a reef at Seven Stones, 16 miles from Lands End, breaking its back. Some 117,000 tons of Kuwaiti crude oil spewed out, threatening wide-scale pollution. For three days, waves of RN and RAF aircraft – including the Hunters from Chivenor – bombed the wreck with napalm and rockets. (RAF Chivenor)

Sixteen Hunters and two Meteors are seen during the flypast tour of the towns of Devon and Cornwall on 1 April 1968 to commemorate the 50th anniversary of the RAF. (RAF Chivenor)

Hunter F.6 XG225 of No. 63 (Reserve) Squadron taxying past the crowd-line during Friends Day at Chivenor, 8 August 1973. The squadron later flew Hawks at Chivenor. (Author)

The classic lines of Hunter F.6 XK149 of No. 79 (Reserve) Squadron are apparent over the Newport area of Barnstaple, 1969. (RAF Chivenor)

Auster 5 G-AJXC of the Puffin Aero Club at Wrafton. Following wartime use as TJ343, it was owned by the club's director and flying instructor, Maurice Looker, from March 1953 to November 1965. (George Raby)

Student nurse Sheelagh Glover is pleased following her solo flight in the North Devon Flying Club's Auster Aerocrat, G-AJEA, May 1952. With Walter Bond, the club's secretary (on the left), is Maurice Looker. The aircraft was lost when it ditched off Lundy in August 1955. (N.D. Museum)

The air link to Lundy Island was revived on 15 August 1950, when an Auster of the Aero Club was able to make the first landing since the war. The club's Dragon Rapide, G-AKNY, is seen on the island at about this time. (RAF Chivenor)

261	The Puffin · Aero Club · DEVONAIR LIMITED	Passenger Ticket	Nº	23

Place of Issue	*Wrafton Gate*	Date of Issue	*4/9/54.*	Issued by	*illegible*

Name of Passenger	*Mr & Mrs Williams.*

Aerodrome of Departure :	*Chivenor / Lundy.*	Agreed Stopping Place(s) (if any)
Aerodrome of Destination :	*Lundy / Chivenor*	

Date of Flight :	Outward. *4/9/54.*	Return *4/9/54.*

Charter Fare :	*£6*

Name and Address of Carriers :	**DEVONAIR LIMITED** The North Devon Air Centre, Wrafton Gate, Braunton, North Devon.

A ticket issued to Mr and Mrs Williams by Devonair Limited for a return trip to Lundy Island on 4 September 1954. The cost was £6. (Braunton Museum)

Young people unload supplies on Lundy Island from the North Devon Flying Club's Auster, G-AJXC, 1950s. The name 'Kupke' on the baskets is that of a local baker in Braunton village. (RAF Chivenor)

The bad weather has failed to dampen the curiosity of some of the 6,000 people attending Chivenor's first At Home Day, 15 September 1945. A static display comprising Spitfires, Mosquitos, an Oxford and a mass flypast were the highlights of the afternoon. (RAF Chivenor)

With a little ingenuity, these boys satisfy their youthful curiosity to examine a Venom FB.1 of the Fighter Weapons School from Leconfield during the At Home Day, September 1956. The event was officially opened by Air Cdre Sir Frank Whittle. (Frank Davis)

Chivenor Air Days were always eagerly anticipated and well attended. Visitors at the 1964 event are seen inspecting the variety of aircraft on display. (RAF Chivenor)

The first International Air Day was held in 1968, with contributions from France, Belgium, Germany and the USAF and Royal Navy. A smaller static display included a Vampire, Javelin and a Lightning trainer. (RAF Chivenor)

The finale of the 1971 Air Day was a thirty-eight aircraft flypast over the airfield. Some of the participating Hunters are visible in this line-up, awaiting their crews. (Author)

A sight never to be repeated: Meteors and Hunter F.6s, T.7s, FGA.9s and FR.10s lined up on Runway 16/34 during the 1970 Air Day. Most of the aircraft later took part in a mass tactical formation flypast. (RAF Chivenor)

Demonstrating their allegiance to the Chivenor-based training unit, thirty-six Hunters in a perfect formation during the 1970 Air Day. (Author)

Enthusiastic crowds flock to the well-organized Air Day, July 1968. Of interest is the new ATC complex, which moved to its present position adjoining Runway 28/10 in April 1986. (Author)

Airmen of No. 1 (Eng) Squadron are inspected by the AOC, No. 11 Group, AVM I.G. Broom, June 1969. The CO is Gp Capt G.M. Hermitage. (RAF Chivenor)

The OCU also ran a Forward Air Controllers' Course and was issued with a handful of Chipmunk T.10s to provide training for officers of the three services to control air strikes. This aircraft served with the FAC Flight from April 1968 to July 1973. (MAP)

The airmen's Christmas dinner, December 1969. Officers and SNCOs continue the tradition of serving the other ranks. (RAF Chivenor)

Hunter F.74Bs of the Singapore Operational Training Flight, May 1973. Both aircraft were ex-RAF Hunter F.6s. (Avia Press)

Hunter FR.10 XE596 returns from a sortie during the St Mawgan detachment, June 1969. This aircraft crashed in Germany the following year. (RAF Chivenor)

To allow Chivenor's runways to be resurfaced in June and July 1969, most of the aircraft and crews were detached to St Mawgan. This was the OCU's Detachment HQ. (RAF Chivenor)

This Meteor T.7 spent two periods of service at Chivenor, first as an advanced trainer and then as a target tug. It was presented to Staverton Airport in 1976. (Author)

The Towed Target Flight, comprising three Meteor F(TT).8s and a T.7, February 1970. The white building in the background is a newly completed drugs manufacturing factory at Wrafton. (RAF Chivenor)

Meteor F(TT)8 WH286 of the Towed Target Flight wearing the conspicuous colour scheme befitting its role, August 1969. (MAP)

Groundcrew of 'A' Flight, No. 1 Squadron, in 1970. The flight commander, Flt Lt Don Marshall, is to the right. He was killed in a Hunter crash the following year. (RAF Chivenor)

In November 1970, Flt Lt Griffiss became the last pilot to be trained for a front-line Hunter squadron. He is seen celebrating the occasion with the station commander, Gp Capt Hermitage. (RAF Chivenor)

Surrounded by the first stages of a £17 million rebuilding programme, the Flying Wing HQ and ATC stands virtually intact, February 1980. The Whirlwinds operated temporarily from the ASP in front of the hangars, which await re-cladding. (RAF Chivenor)

Some of the wartime buildings on the technical site had been demolished by February 1980, six months before the station officially re-opened. (RAF Chivenor)

With much of the major rebuilding and refurbishment work completed, one ASP appears to be in use by the Hawks of No. 63(R) Squadron. (RAF Chivenor)

This is the first of the six Hawk T.1s of No. 63(R) Squadron/No. 2 TWU to transfer from Brawdy, 1 August 1980. The TWU began course training the following week. (Author)

AVM Peter Latham, CB, AFC, AOC No. 11 Group, is greeted on arrival at Chivenor on 1 August 1980 by the station commander, Wg Cdr Roger Austin, DFC. (Author)

Hawk T.1 XX334 of No. 1 Training Squadron, August 1981. The unit had formed at Chivenor on 1 April 1981 and was renumbered as 151(R) Squadron the following September. (Author)

Crews prepare a Hawk T.1 of No. 151(R) Squadron for a sortie, 1982. The normal task of the squadron was to teach students previously qualified on the Hawk the art of air combat, weaponry and tactical low flying. (Author)

Hunter F.1s on the northern apron, July 1956. At the end of the line-up are a Meteor of the TT Flight and a Mosquito from Pembrey. (J.D. Rawlings)

The northern apron with Hawk T.1s makes an interesting comparison, March 1982. Students flew about seventy hours during their intensive four-month course at Chivenor. (Author)

The TWU trained nearly a hundred pilots per year and provided fighter experience for up to seventy-five navigators. These are Hawk T.1s of No. 63(R) Squadron in 1982. (Author)

This fly-past of eight No. 151(R) Squadron Hawks in June 1982 is celebrating the victory in the Falkland Islands, with the tail codes arranged to spell the station name. (RAF Chivenor)

Two Hawks flying over the bridge spanning the River Torridge at Bideford in 1988, a year after it was opened officially. (RAF Chivenor)

A 1920s-style party, August 1983. The WRAF officers' dresses at least look authentic! (Baths Photographic)

In July 1990, some of the Hawks began to wear large, stylized squadron badges on their fins. Hawk T.1A XX289 of No. 63(R) Squadron is seen here wearing the short-lived yellow disc, which was removed to conform with the tail insignia of No. 151(R) Squadron. (Author)

Two Hawks were applied with special markings to commemorate the station's fiftieth anniversary. XX278 is pictured with No. 63(R) Squadron's yellow logotype on a black background in November 1990. (Author)

In February 1987, an ex-Royal Navy Hunter GA.11 was obtained in flying condition and adorned with the markings of the resident flying units. It was eventually passed into store at Shawbury. (Author)

Following service at RAF Valley, Hunter F.6 XF509/8708M was transferred to Chivenor in April 1983 and mounted into position at the main gate in October 1990. It was sold with the closure of the station in 1995. (Author)

A MiG-23ML and MiG-29 of the Czech Air Force are escorted by two Hawks for the 1991 Air Day. The event was virtually rained off and the two MiGs did not fly because of technical problems. (RAF Chivenor)

During the first of two conspicuity trials held at Chivenor to determine a definitive paint scheme for the RAF's Hawks, XX255 was temporarily resprayed in an overall matt black scheme in October 1991. (RAF Chivenor)

A three-year programme to upgrade Chivenor's Hawks by re-wiring the wings to accept AIM-9L Sidewinder missiles was completed in May 1986. The war-roled Hawk T.1As were also resprayed in a mixed grey paint scheme. (BAe)

A surprise visitor to Chivenor was British Airways Concorde G-BOAG, which was persuaded to carry out a roller landing during an air test, March 1990. (RAF Chivenor)

The last of the accommodation huts to be dismantled, 1992. This one originally formed part of 'C' Lines. (Author)

The wooden accommodation huts were finally demolished some forty-six years after they were built! (Author)

Wearing distinctive Cobra fin markings, Hawk T.1A XX337 of No. 92(R) Squadron has a practice bomb carrier mounted on the wing pylon. (RAF Chivenor)

The 1992 'Options For Change' policy resulted in a transfer to RAF Support Command and the renumbering of No. 2 TWU as No. 7 FTS. In September 1992, Nos 63 and 151 Squadrons were renumbered as 19 and 92 Squadrons respectively. Hawk T.1A XX219 was specifically chosen to represent No. 19(R) Squadron because of the 'last three' of its airframe serial number. (RAF Chivenor)

Over the years, many flying units were detached to Chivenor for periods of operational training. One such unit was 509 TFS/10 TFW, USAF from Alconbury flying A-10A Thunderbolt IIs, one of which (77-0254) is seen in June 1991. (Author)

'E' Flight, No. 275 (ASR) Squadron was detached to Chivenor with Sycamore HR.14 helicopters from June 1957 to November 1958. With an establishment of eight aircrew and fourteen airmen, the flight was commanded by Flt Lt George 'Kiwi' Francis, DFC, AFC. (George Francis)

Sycamore HR.14 XE317 of 'E' Flight, No. 275 Squadron, 'wet' winching off Ilfracombe harbour. The flight became operational on 25 June 1957 when it rescued the crew member of a Royal Navy Firefly. (George Francis)

During its eighteen-month stay at Chivenor, 'E' Flight answered over fifty emergency calls. Here Sycamore HR.14 XJ364 comes in to land. (George Francis)

'A' Flight, No. 22 Squadron, was established at Chivenor on 8 November 1958 with Whirlwind HAR.2s. This Whirlwind, XJ763, was converted to an HAR.10 in 1960 and eventually sold to a buyer in Texas in April 1982. (RAF Chivenor)

A 'Flying Bedstead'? Whirlwind HAR.2 XJ433 carries out its own crazy experiments in VTOL flying for an Air Day. The last Whirlwind HAR.2 was returned to Westland in August 1962. (RAF Chivenor)

Turbine-powered Whirlwind HAR.10s were delivered to 'A' Flight in 1961 and frequently practised wet dinghy drill with the rescue lifeboats and coastguards. (RAF Chivenor)

One of the hazards of low flying! Whirlwind HAR.10 XJ410 crashed into the River Torridge at Little America near Bideford after hitting HT cables, 21 September 1965. (RAF Chivenor)

Helicopter operations, winter 1962. Chivenor's Whirlwinds carried out 176 sorties during Operation 'Snowdrop', bringing food and supplies to stranded hamlets and farms. (RAF Chivenor)

On 20 February 1971, XJ426 suffered an engine failure and crashed on Braunton Burrows. It is seen here being airlifted back to Chivenor by a RN Sea King from Culdrose. Six months later the same Whirlwind ditched off Lundy and was lost. (RNAS Culdrose)

Whirlwind helicopters were criticized for being too slow and incapable of sophisticated night flying, but were remembered with affection by those who flew them. (RAF Chivenor)

The last active RAF Whirlwinds were officially retired from SAR service with 'A' Flight on 30 November 1981, having been scrambled over 2,000 times and rescued or assisted 1,600 people. (Author)

The Wessex HC.2 enjoyed an increased range and payload, and a heavier lift capability, than its predecessor. (Author)

In fourteen years of service, the Wessex HC.2s of 'A' Flight were called out to 1,822 emergencies. From October 1989, operations were usually restricted to daylight hours. (Author)

'A' Flight moved to a new, purpose-built domestic and operations complex at the north end of the airfield in April 1980, for which a hangar was transported from Wattisham. (Author)

One of 'A' Flight's Wessex HC.2s – a 'paraffin budgie' – is scrambled to rescue another holidaymaker, 1982. (Author)

With their greater range and night capability, the Sea Kings of 'A' Flight enabled a return to a twenty-four hour standby at Chivenor, thus enhancing SAR cover. (OC, No. 22 Squadron)

'A' Flight, No. 22 Squadron, upgraded to the Sea King HAR.3 on 30 June 1994 when the aircraft and personnel of 'B' Flight, No. 202 Squadron, were transferred from Brawdy. (OC, No. 22 Squadron)

The spacious interior of the Sea King is evident as it is flown off the North Devon coast with co-pilot Flt Lt 'Windy' Miller in the left-hand seat. (OC, No. 22 Squadron)

The Sea King carries a crew of four. Typical of such crews are, left to right, Flt Lt 'Windy' Miller (captain), Sgt Jamie Eden-Hamilton (winchman), Flt Lt Hayden Williams (co-pilot), and MAEOp Steve Ward (radar/winch operator). (OC, No. 22 Squadron)

The fortieth anniversary of SAR operations at Chivenor was celebrated on 17 February 1995 with a unique line-up comprising Sea King HAR.3 XZ595, Wessex HC.2 XR520, and civilian Whirlwind HAR.10 XJ763/G-BKHA. (OC, No. 22 Squadron)

A Cadet TX.3 glider, XE802 of No. 624 VGS, June 1981. (Author)

About to touch down following a successful familiarization flight for an ATC cadet is Sedburgh TX.1 WB973 of No. 624 VGS. (Author)

The first Venture T.2s were delivered to No. 624 VGS in April 1983. XZ558 is seen at the Air Day in July 1988. (Author)

Symbolizing the Air Training Corp's role of providing basic flying training and passenger flying for its cadets is a Chipmunk from No. 4 AEF at Exeter and a Venture T.2 of No. 624 VGS. (RAF Chivenor)

1991 was a year of triple celebrations for the gliding school: the arrival of three new Vigilant T.1 motor gliders in May, a move to new accommodation, and the award of a flight safety trophy. (Author)

Twenty Hawks from No. 7 FTS rehearse for the D-Day '50' formation, May 1994. (RAF Chivenor)

Hawk T.1 XX231 of No. 19(R) Squadron was the reserve aircraft for the 1994 airshow season. It is seen on final approach, April 1994. (Author)

To mark Chivenor's final airshow season, Hawk T.1 XX178 of No. 92(R) Squadron was resprayed in the unit's traditional royal blue colour scheme and flown by Flt Lt Dave Stobie. (Author)

By 1992, the old ATC tower has gone and work is about to commence on the new office accommodation in front of the hangars. No. 7 FTS took prospective pilots from basic flying training and trained them to become fast-jet fighter pilots. The students were awarded their 'wings' upon completion of the 100-hour fast-jet and tactical weapons course. (RAF Chivenor)

In October 1992 the Hawks from RAF Valley began to use Chivenor as a forward operating base for weapons training on the Pembrey ranges. Among the first of the Hawks to be detached was XX351 of No. 2 Squadron/4 FTS. (Author)

Returning from a range weapons sortie is Hawk T.1A XX199 of No. 74(R) Squadron at Valley, April 1993. The week-long rotational detachment usually comprised six aircraft. (Author)

The last Hawk to be detached from Valley for weapons training was XX317 of No. 208(R) Squadron, seen departing from Chivenor on 14 March 1995. (Author)

Sqn Ldr Paul Adams is strapped in by Cpl Colin Scaife before departing for Valley on 17 March 1995, bringing an end to fifteen years of Hawk operations at Chivenor. (Author)

Parked under camouflaged netting, a Harrier GR.7 is prepared for flight during Exercise 'Hill Foil', May 1995. (Phil Spencer)

The last two Hawks to leave Chivenor were XX158 of No. 19(R) Squadron and XX204 of No. 92(R) Squadron, 17 March 1995. The latter was the final Hawk to be delivered to the RAF, arriving on 17 March 1982, and leaving thirteen years later to the day! (Author)

Two Harriers from No. 3 Squadron Laarbruch, about to depart Runway 28/10 during Exercise 'Hill Foil'. The light grey scheme of the nearest aircraft was applied for operations over northern Iraq. (Phil Spencer)

About to commence a rolling vertical landing at Chivenor during Exercise 'Hill Foil', this Harrier (ZG859) of No. 4 Squadron wears the special tail scheme of black, gold and red. (Author)

RAF Chivenor, 1985. Few airfields could boast two ATC towers; the eastern end of the runway was also obscured by the hangars, resulting in a television monitor being installed to allow controllers to observe the approach. Runway 10/28 (6,012 yds) is bisected by 16/34 (4,434 yds) and the disused runway. (RAF Chivenor)

Acknowledgements

Having taken many years to accumulate a collection of photographs covering the period 1940–95 it was difficult to make a final selection for inclusion in this book. Many of these photographs came from private collections. Some, however, came from official sources and every effort has been made by the author and the publishers to trace owners of copyright material. I am therefore grateful to the following for their generous support:

Andy Anderson • Sqn Ldr Maurice Biggs • British Aviation Review
AVM A.A. Case • Gp Capt Norman Curtis • Frank Davis • Sqn Ldr J.A.
Forrest • Flt Lt 'Kiwi' Francis • R.L. Knight Collection • John Rawlings
Sqn Ldr John Harvey • Bob Hillard • Ken Hogbin • Len Lineker • Wg Cdr
D.T.M. Lumsden • Wg Cdr K.W. Mackenzie • Bill Parsons • Gp Capt H.P.
Pleasance • Jeff Rounce • Colin Sloan • Phil Spencer of the British Aviation
Research Group and *Roundel* magazine • G.P. Young

I must thank my wife Anne and my mother-in-law Audrey for being subjected yet again to my temporary distraction. Thanks also to 'Dinger' Bell, for supplying photographs and copious amounts of home-made beer; to Marcus Bath, whose photographic skills made my impossible requirements a reality; to Alison Mills of the Museum of North Devon and Les Franklin of the Barnstaple Athenaeum; to Flt Lts John Doonan and 'Windy' Miller of RAF Chivenor; and to all those I am unable to name personally because of a lack of space.

BRITAIN IN OLD PHOTOGRAPHS

To order any of these titles please telephone Littlehampton Book Services on 01903 721596

Scunthorpe, *D Taylor*
Skegness, *W Kime*
Around Skegness, *W Kime*

LONDON

Balham and Tooting, *P Loobey*
Crystal Palace, Penge & Anerley, *M Scott*
Greenwich and Woolwich, *K Clark*
Hackney: A Second Selection, *D Mander*
Lewisham and Deptford, *J Coulter*
Lewisham and Deptford: A Second Selection, *J Coulter*
Streatham, *P Loobey*
Around Whetstone and North Finchley, *J Heathfield*
Woolwich, *B Evans*

MONMOUTHSHIRE

Chepstow and the River Wye, *A Rainsbury*
Monmouth and the River Wye, *Monmouth Museum*

NORFOLK

Great Yarmouth, *M Teun*
Norwich, *M Colman*
Wymondham and Attleborough, *P Yaxley*

NORTHAMPTONSHIRE

Around Stony Stratford, *A Lambert*

NOTTINGHAMSHIRE

Arnold and Bestwood, *M Spick*
Arnold and Bestwood: A Second Selection, *M Spick*
Changing Face of Nottingham, *G Oldfield*
Mansfield, *Old Mansfield Society*
Around Newark, *T Warner*
Nottingham: 1944–1974, *D Whitworth*
Sherwood Forest, *D Ottewell*
Victorian Nottingham, *M Payne*

OXFORDSHIRE

Around Abingdon, *P Horn*
Banburyshire, *M Barnett & S Gosling*
Burford, *A Jewell*
Around Didcot and the Hagbournes, *B Lingham*
Garsington, *M Gunther*
Around Henley-on-Thames, *S Ellis*
Oxford: The University, *J Rhodes*
Thame to Watlington, *N Hood*
Around Wallingford, *D Beasley*
Witney, *T Worley*
Around Witney, *C Mitchell*
Witney District, *T Worley*
Around Woodstock, *J Bond*

POWYS

Brecon, *Brecknock Museum*
Welshpool, *E Bredsdorff*

SHROPSHIRE

Shrewsbury, *D Trumper*
Whitchurch to Market Drayton, *M Morris*

SOMERSET

Bath, *J Hudson*
Bridgwater and the River Parrett, *R Fitzhugh*
Bristol, *D Moorcroft & N Campbell-Sharp*
Changing Face of Keynsham,
    B Lowe & M Whitehead

Chard and Ilminster, *G Gosling & F Huddy*
Crewkerne and the Ham Stone Villages,
    G Gosling & F Huddy
Around Keynsham and Saltford, *B Lowe & T Brown*
Midsomer Norton and Radstock, *C Howell*
Somerton, Ilchester and Langport, *G Gosling & F Huddy*
Taunton, *N Chipchase*
Around Taunton, *N Chipchase*
Wells, *C Howell*
Weston-Super-Mare, *S Poole*
Around Weston-Super-Mare, *S Poole*
West Somerset Villages, *K Houghton & L Thomas*

STAFFORDSHIRE

Aldridge, *J Farrow*
Bilston, *E Rees*
Black Country Transport: Aviation, *A Brew*
Around Burton upon Trent, *G Sowerby & R Farman*
Bushbury, *A Chatwin, M Mills & E Rees*
Around Cannock, *M Mills & S Belcher*
Around Leek, *R Poole*
Lichfield, *H Clayton & K Simmons*
Around Pattingham and Wombourne, *M Griffiths,
    P Leigh & M Mills*
Around Rugeley, *T Randall & J Anslow*
Smethwick, *J Maddison*
Stafford, *J Anslow & T Randall*
Around Stafford, *J Anslow & T Randall*
Stoke-on-Trent, *I Lawley*
Around Tamworth, *R Sulima*
Around Tettenhall and Codsall, *M Mills*
Tipton, Wednesbury and Darlaston, *R Pearson*
Walsall, *D Gilbert & M Lewis*
Wednesbury, *I Bott*
West Bromwich, *R Pearson*

SUFFOLK

Ipswich: A Second Selection, *D Kindred*
Around Ipswich, *D Kindred*
Around Mildenhall, *C Dring*
Southwold to Aldeburgh, *H Phelps*
Around Woodbridge, *H Phelps*

SURREY

Cheam and Belmont, *P Berry*
Croydon, *S Bligh*
Dorking and District, *K Harding*
Around Dorking, *A Jackson*
Around Epsom, *P Berry*
Farnham: A Second Selection, *J Parratt*
Around Haslemere and Hindhead, *T Winter & G Collyer*
Richmond, *Richmond Local History Society*
Sutton, *P Berry*

SUSSEX

Arundel and the Arun Valley, *J Godfrey*
Bishopstone and Seaford, *P Pople & P Berry*
Brighton and Hove, *J Middleton*
Brighton and Hove: A Second Selection, *J Middleton*
Around Crawley, *M Goldsmith*
Hastings, *P Haines*
Hastings: A Second Selection, *P Haines*
Around Haywards Heath, *J Middleton*
Around Heathfield, *A Gillet & B Russell*
Around Heathfield: A Second Selection,
    A Gillet & B Russell
High Weald, *B Harwood*
High Weald: A Second Selection, *B Harwood*
Horsham and District, *T Wales*

Lewes, *J Middleton*
RAF Tangmere, *A Saunders*
Around Rye, *A Dickinson*
Around Worthing, *S White*

WARWICKSHIRE

Along the Avon from Stratford to Tewkesbury, *J Jeremiah*
Bedworth, *J Burton*
Coventry, *D McGrory*
Around Coventry, *D McGrory*
Nuneaton, *S Clews & S Vaughan*
Around Royal Leamington Spa, *J Cameron*
Around Royal Leamington Spa: A Second Selection,
    J Cameron
Around Warwick, *R Booth*

WESTMORLAND

Eden Valley, *J Marsh*
Kendal, *M & P Duff*
South Westmorland Villages, *J Marsh*
Westmorland Lakes, *J Marsh*

WILTSHIRE

Around Amesbury, *P Daniels*
Chippenham and Lacock, *A Wilson & M Wilson*
Around Corsham and Box, *A Wilson & M Wilson*
Around Devizes, *D Buxton*
Around Highworth, *G Tanner*
Around Highworth and Faringdon, *G Tanner*
Around Malmesbury, *A Wilson*
Marlborough: A Second Selection, *P Colman*
Around Melksham,
    Melksham and District Historical Association
Nadder Valley, *R. Sawyer*
Salisbury, *P Saunders*
Salisbury: A Second Selection, *P Daniels*
Salisbury: A Third Selection, *P Daniels*
Around Salisbury, *P Daniels*
Swindon: A Third Selection, *The Swindon Society*
Swindon: A Fourth Selection, *The Swindon Society*
Trowbridge, *M Marshman*
Around Wilton, *P Daniels*
Around Wootton Bassett, Cricklade and Purton, *T Sharp*

WORCESTERSHIRE

Evesham to Bredon, *F Archer*
Around Malvern, *K Smith*
Around Pershore, *M Dowty*
Redditch and the Needle District, *R Saunders*
Redditch: A Second Selection, *R Saunders*
Around Tenbury Wells, *D Green*
Worcester, *M Dowty*
Around Worcester, *R Jones*
Worcester in a Day, *M Dowty*
Worcestershire at Work, *R Jones*

YORKSHIRE

Huddersfield: A Second Selection, *H Wheeler*
Huddersfield: A Third Selection, *H Wheeler*
Leeds Road and Rail, *R Vickers*
Pontefract, *R van Riel*
Scarborough, *D Coggins*
Scarborough's War Years, *R Percy*
Skipton and the Dales, *Friends of the Craven Museum*
Around Skipton-in-Craven, *Friends of the Craven Museum*
Yorkshire Wolds, *I & M Sumner*